Today I Choose

Daily Intentions to Guide You Through Your Life

Volume 2

Melissa Bingham

Cover design by Marsha Craig.

For my Mom and Dad.

Thank you for being exactly who you are and helping to make me who I am.

Thank you to my biggest fans…
Dave, Molly, Cooper and Tallulah.

Thank you to the support of my tribe in our
Everyday Living with Intention community.

A MESSAGE TO YOU, THE READER

Volume II! 365 new daily intentions.

Welcome to *Today I Choose*. My intention over the last eight years has been to live every day on purpose; to use the spiritual practice of setting a daily intention to help guide me through my life. I'm so happy to be sharing this daily practice with you in Volume 2 of *Today I Choose: Daily Intentions to Guide You Through Your Life.*

What is Intention?

To intend is to have a course of action…as one's purpose. Intention, therefore, is the act of having a determined (or predetermined) end. It is the spark, the kernel, the seed behind your purpose. It is the riverbed directing the flow of water or the genetics before the physical expression – the action of becoming without being the thing it becomes.

Each intention has a will. But water no more thinks the direction of the riverbed than you think your intention. Both just flow. Both are felt.

Intentions come from your heart; they come from your soul. The first step in setting your intention is to connect to your heart. Slow down, breathe, get quiet, and listen to what your heart and soul whisper.

The habit of setting a daily intention is a powerful spiritual practice. I've made it a part of my daily ritual for years. Before I started, I had been doing a lot of study and testing around the power of intention; not in the "law of attraction... I'm going to manifest everything I want" way. But more in the, "I'm co-creating with my Divine and I'm going to live actively in that practice" way. For me, intention is a message to Spirit. It's me saying, "Use me. I'm ready. I'm working with you, not against you." So by choosing every day, I'm sending a message to the Universe: I'm ready to co-create with you.

This daily practice has changed my life. I start each day by making a choice as to how I'm going to live. I set an intention for how I will look at the world, how I will act in the world, what I might feel, and how I want to show up for my family, friends, and self. Some days, I'm true to my choice. Other days, I fall flat on my face within minutes of choosing.

My invitation to you with this book is to simply start – to start living your life with intention and as a result may you find yourself in active co-creation with Source.

With love and intention,

Melissa

PS… My intention is to get this book out into the world, flaws and all. And, there may be places where an intention is repeated and that's because I may have needed the same intention on a different day for a different reason. May this book serve you.

How to Use this Book

This book is designed to be used in a variety of
ways:

- **Daily Guidance**…by following along each
  day and to see how the intention I set
  applies to your day. Take the daily
  intention as your own or…

- **Daily Inspiration**…by using each daily
  intention as inspiration for your own
  intention. Heck, turn it into your own
  journal! Follow the below three steps for
  setting your daily intention, then write
  your own intention underneath the one on
  each page.
  1.   Connect to your heart. Slow down,
        breathe, feel and listen.
  2.   Allow your intention to bubble up
        inside of you from your heart, from
        your belly. (Not down from your
        head, thinking it)
  3.   Speak it, write it down, and be
        witnessed.

- **Intuitive Guidance**…by using this book as an oracle (a way of receiving information) to find inspiration:

  1. Hold the closed book between your two hands.
  2. Ask in your mind or out loud, whichever feels more comfortable, "What do I need to know today?"
  3. Then open the book and read the page to see what the message is.

However you decide to use this book,
may it lead you to living a more intentional life!

Today
I
Choose

January 1

Today I choose to anchor my year by deepening my daily intention practice.

January 2

Today I choose to trust my intuition
and follow its guidance.

January 3

Today I choose to surround myself
with beauty

.

January 4

Today I choose to stay in beginner's mind:
to be teachable, to be coachable.

January 5

Today I choose to honor the Divinity and wholeness in everyone-- even when they appear to be the exact opposite.

January 6

Today I choose to be flexible.

January 7

Today I choose to create a fun, sacred day
of ritual, visioning and dreaming
with my family.

January 8

Today I choose to listen to my body and give it what it needs... rest and water.

January 9

Today I choose to find joy in the details.

January 10

Today I choose to trust in the perfect
timing of everything.

January 11

Today I choose to enjoy the spaciousness in my day and resist the need to fill every moment with doing.

January 12

Today I choose to allow my inner Muse
to light the way.

January 13

Today I choose to forgive myself for
slipping back into old habits and simply
make a different, conscious choice
in this new day.

January 14

Today I choose to be willing to ask for
what I need —
physically, emotionally and spiritually.

January 15

Today I choose to trust in the
power of prayer.

January 16

Today I choose to do things that nourish
my mind, body and spirit.

January 17

Today I choose to have patience and compassion with myself and others.

January 18

Today I choose to be a fierce stand of love
for the people I care about the most.

January 19

Today I choose to cherish every breath.

January 20

Today I choose to focus on what I love the most-- my family, my friends and holding space for people to help them connect to their Divine Truth.

January 21

Today I choose to stand in my power.

January 22

Today I choose to connect to people, places and things that inspire me.

January 23

Today I choose to let compassion be my guide.

January 24

Today I choose to release over-responsibility for things and remember I only have to do my part.

January 25

Today I choose gratitude for amazing friends that support me in so many different ways, that make me laugh and are there with a shoulder to cry on when I need it.

January 26

Today I choose faith.

January 27

Today I choose to find the sacred third option even though right now things seem to be this or that.

January 28

Today I choose to listen and really hear what the other person is saying without needing to form a response or rebuttal.

January 29

Today I choose to be gentle with myself.

January 30

Today I choose self-care first.

January 31

Today I choose to be happy.

February 1

Today I choose to unplug and listen to my
voice instead of all of the
noise around me.

February 2

Today I choose to listen to my body.

February 3

Today I choose to embrace possibility.

February 4

Today I choose to trust in the
Divine unfoldment of Life.

February 5

Today I choose to bring things to order
and to put more structure in
place for my work.

February 6

Today I choose gratitude for my breath.

February 7

Today I choose to feel into, transmute and release the root cause of the frustration I am feeling with ease and grace.

February 8

Today I choose to look for signs.

MELISSA BINGHAM

February 9

Today I choose to be gentle
in every interaction.

February 10

Today I choose to remember that the Universe is always supporting me.

February 11

Today I choose to create something new.

February 12

Today I choose to trust in the power of Love.

February 13

Today I choose to embrace this week
that is full of possibility.

February 14

Today I choose love and compassion —
even when it's hard.

February 15

Today I choose to use my gifts and talents
in service of others to help
them shine brightly.

February 16

Today I choose to be silly, to talk in funny voices with my kids (and maybe adults too) and laugh and laugh and laugh-- it's time to LIGHTen up!!

February 17

Today I choose to dance in the rain.

February 18

Today I choose to get out of my own way
and let the Divine guide my every step.

February 19

Today I choose to trust that everything is working out perfectly.

February 20

Today I choose to celebrate the funny, creative, smart, handsome men in my life.

February 21

Today I choose to do one thing at a time.

February 22

Today I choose to stop seeking answers outside of myself.

February 23

Today I choose to start again —
as many times as it takes.

February 24

Today I choose to let Grace guide
my hand and my word.

February 25

Today I choose to be patient
with everyone and everything.

February 26

Today I choose to stop seeing problems and start seeing perfection.

February 27

Today I choose to take my cues
from my body.

February 28

Today I choose to breathe, just breathe.

March 1

Today I choose to cherish myself.

March 2

Today I choose to let go of the story that life is stressful and hard right now.

March 3

Today I choose to be of service.

March 4

Today I choose to allow everything to flow with ease and grace.

March 5

Today I choose to let go with Grace.

March 6

Today I choose gratitude for my tribe.

March 7

Today I choose ease, grace and
style in my travels.

March 8

Today I choose to roll with
whatever comes my way.

March 9

Today I choose to see the
abundance all around me.

March 10

Today I choose to remember that even though I'm not "working" as much as I'm use to or would like to, I'm doing my "work" by the way I am living my life and showing up in every interaction, conversation and activity.

March 11

Today I choose to be kind to myself.

March 12

Today I choose to talk less
and listen more.

March 13

Today I choose to recognize
the support all around me.

March 14

Today I choose to allow creativity
to flow through me.

March 15

Today I choose to connect to my dreams.

March 16

Today I choose to lean into the frustration
I'm feeling and ask it what messages
it has for me.

March 17

Today I choose to celebrate my wealth... in
health, in love, in friends and family, in
time and space, in beauty, in joy
and in financial abundance.

March 18

Today I choose to dream up amazing possibilities for our life and plant some seeds toward making them come true.

March 19

Today I choose to be kind to myself.

March 20

Today I choose to weed my mental garden
so that new possibilities
can spring forward.

March 21

Today I choose to stop bullying myself
and recognize that those people who are
bullying me and my family are acting out
of their own pain and fear. I choose to cut
any energetic chords, agreements or holds
that they have on me or my family. I
choose to surround myself and my family
in a bubble of Love and Divine protection.
I completely release everyone into their
own experience knowing it has
no hold on me.

March 22

Today I choose to unplug and turn within.

March 23

Today I choose patience.

March 24

Today I choose patience, again.

March 25

Today I choose to embrace the unknown.

March 26

Today I choose to have a
clear, focused mind.

March 27

Today I choose to no longer let
past stories define me.

March 28

Today I choose to be playful.

March 29

Today I choose to focus.

March 30

Today I choose to give myself the gift of spaciousness and a technology break.

March 31

Today I choose to embark
on a new adventure.

April 1

Today I choose to roll with the tides.

April 2

Today I choose to move at a turtle's pace.

April 3

Today I choose to trust in Divine timing.

April 4

Today I choose to Love fiercely.

April 5

Today I choose to enjoy the moment.

April 6

Today I chose to celebrate Life.

April 7

Today I choose to move gently
through my day.

April 8

Today I choose to enjoy
getting caught up on life at home.

April 9

Today I choose to rest and
know my wholeness.

April 10

Today I choose peace in my body
and in my mind.

April 11

Today I choose to be patient with myself, let my body heal and give it the rest it needs without judgement.

April 12

Today I choose to have some fun!

April 13

Today I choose to let Love
guide my every action.

April 14

Today I choose to be spontaneous.

April 15

Today I choose to do what's in front of me
and trust the rest will get done
in perfect time.

April 16

Today I choose to have
fun with my family!

April 17

Today I choose to enjoy every breath.

April 18

Today I choose to leap knowing
that the net will appear.

April 19

Today I choose to celebrate the
awesome people around me.

April 20

Today I choose to embrace my passions regardless of what anyone else thinks.

April 21

Today I choose to sink into the spacious,
still moments between the doing.

April 22

Today I choose a renewed commitment to keep in touch with dear friends and family regardless of distance or time zone.

April 23

Today I choose to dance.

April 24

Today I choose to focus on the details.

April 25

Today I choose to see the Truth and
release the illusion.

April 26

Today I choose to be in the room
where it happens.

April 27

Today I choose patience - patience in my thought, my word and my action.

April 28

Today I choose to go at my own pace.

April 29

Today I choose to trust that
today will be easy.

April 30

Today I choose to jump into a bigger pool.

May 1

Today I choose to focus.

May 2

Today (and always) I choose
to lead with Love.

May 3

Today I choose to bring a chapter in our lives to completion with Grace and allow whatever emotions arise to be OK knowing it's all part of the process.

May 4

Today I choose to enjoy flowers,
community and celebration.

May 5

Today I choose to go at a turtle's pace...
slow and steady.

May 6

Today I choose to roll with
the changes around me.

May 7

Today I choose to trust.

May 8

Today I choose to go slowly.

May 9

Today I choose to enjoy
the beauty in nature.

May 10

Today I choose to be fully present
where ever I go.

May 11

Today I choose unabashed J-O-Y.

May 12

Today I choose to enjoy
all of life's chapters.

May 13

Today I choose to bask the sunshine.

May 14

Today I choose to honor Motherhood
in all of her forms.

May 15

Today I choose to look at life from
a different perspective.

May 16

Today I choose to listen to my body and
rest as much as it needs.

May 17

Today I choose to get out of my own way.

May 18

Today I choose to look every person I see
in the eye and affirm their
wholeness and Divinity.

May 19

Today I choose to tend to what's right in front of me.

May 20

Today I choose to tune into
my heart's desires.

May 21

Today I choose to follow my heart.

May 22

Today I choose to allow inspiration to flow freely and not judge an idea before it has time to germinate.

May 23

Today I choose to march to my own drum.

May 24

Today I choose to lean into fear and
ask what it wants me to know.

May 25

Today I choose to invite ease to flow
through my day.

May 26

Today I choose to have fun with everything I'm doing.

May 27

Today I choose to radiate positive energy.

May 28

Today I choose to be peace in action.

May 29

Today I choose to pay attention and consciously choose the words that I speak.

May 30

Today I choose to be patient —
very, very patient.

May 31

Today I chose to rise above the daily drama that seemingly keeps appearing and hold the high watch to see the Divine perfection in all that is unfolding.

June 1

Today I choose to speak Truth.

June 2

Today I choose to clear away the lingering
mental clutter that clouds my mind so
I can do what I'm here to do.

June 3

Today I choose to be inspired by all of the
creative people of all ages around me.

June 4

Today I choose to appreciate
every single moment of the day.

June 5

Today I choose to take the high road, to not get mired down in the drama and to know there is a spiritual solution to every "problem".

June 6

Today I choose to be gentle.

June 7

Today I choose to ground myself
with every breath.

June 8

Today I choose to simply enjoy the ride
and not worry about the destination.

June 9

Today I choose to complete another
chapter in life, savoring each moment, and
looking forward to the blank
page before me.

June 10

Today I choose to not take
myself so seriously.

June 11

Today I choose to relax and enjoy
family and friends.

June 12

Today I choose to be present.

June 13

Today I choose to listen to my body
and give it what it needs.

June 14

Today I choose to embrace and love everything just as it is right now. Even if there is room for improvement, I choose gratitude for what is.

June 15

Today I choose to reach out to a friend I haven't spoken to in along time.

June 16

Today I choose to trust that I'm exactly where I'm supposed to be and ask, "What is mine to do here?"

June 17

Today I choose to believe that I truly can do anything I set my heart to do and mind to accomplish, no matter how hard it may seem or how long it may take.

June 18

Today I choose to celebrate the Divine Masculine in everyone.

June 19

Today I choose to try something new.

June 20

Today I choose to pause and remember all that I've done this year and feel into where I'm being called to serve next.

June 21

Today I choose to trust that my day
is unfolding perfectly.

June 22

Today I choose to trust in the eb and flow of energy, money, work, inspiration, and spaciousness and commit to enjoying each movement even when it feels uncomfortable.

June 23

Today I choose to listen for my heart to inform my head before I take action.

June 24

Today I choose to embrace and love my body exactly as it is right now.

June 25

Today I choose to remember that each person is on their own soul path. I choose to allow them to make their own choices. I choose to release any feelings of over-responsible that I may have. I trust that the Divine has their back and mine.

June 26

Today I choose to listen to my heart's desires and follow their lead.

June 27

Today I choose to focus on
building bridges.

June 28

Today I choose to keep asking "what else is possible" when I feel stuck or fearful.

June 29

Today I choose to ask for help and remember I always have the support I need.

June 30

Today I choose to ground myself
and take things slowly.

July 1

Today I choose gratitude for all of the wonderful people in my life.

July 2

Today I choose to recognize my prosperity
in all of its forms.

July 3

Today I choose to look at old issues as if I'm seeing them for the first time and let a beautiful new solution emerge.

July 4

Today I choose to celebrate all of my freedoms and take some time to reflect on places in my life where I hold myself captive to a limiting belief.

July 5

Today I choose to be compassionately
fierce in all I do.

July 6

Today I choose to be open
to new opportunities.

July 7

Today I choose to stay centered in my
heart and follow its lead.

July 8

Today I choose to place my attention on what is working instead of what is not.

July 9

Today I choose to take care of me.

July 10

Today I choose to let go of fear
and focus on Truth.

July 11

Today I choose to surround myself
with positive, healthy people.

July 12

Today I choose to allow my actions to
achieve maximum benefit
with minimal effort.

July 13

Today I choose to let go of the outcome
and trust that everything is
unfolding perfectly.

July 14

Today I choose to listen to my inner wisdom and follow its words.

July 15

Today I choose to stretch my body beyond
what I thought was possible.

July 16

Today I choose to look for inspiration in unlikely places and allow myself to receive the vibrant creative life force around me.

July 17

Today I choose to wipe away the cob webs
(literally and figuratively) so I can
see more clearly.

July 18

Today I choose to re-engage my left brain.
It's been enjoying the summer break!

July 19

Today I choose to ask myself "is this really mine to do" and listen quietly for my soul's answer.

July 20

Today I choose to start my day with Grace, to release fear and judgement and to embrace beautiful new opportunities.

July 21

Today I choose to move through my
emotions and be gentle with myself.

July 22

Today I choose to enjoy where I am.

July 23

Today I choose to allow the heat
to fuel my passion.

July 24

Today I choose to laugh at myself.

July 25

Today I choose to celebrate life.

July 26

Today I choose to stand still in the eye of the storm and know that I am Divinely protected.

July 27

Today I choose to release judgement of how other people do things and allow them to have their own experience.

July 28

Today I choose to keep my self grounded in the present moment. No where else to be, nothing else to do except what is right in front of me --right here, right now.

July 29

Today I choose to anchor myself in Love.

July 30

Today I choose to keep things simple.

July 31

Today I choose to focus on
one moment at a time.

August 1

Today I choose to set
very clear boundaries.

August 2

Today I choose to Trust that all I have to do is my piece (peace) and allow others to do theirs.

August 3

Today I choose to recognize I'm doing my
best even when my
inner perfectionist says otherwise.

August 4

Today I choose to trust myself and my inner guidance above everything else.

August 5

Today I choose to allow change and seek
out the sacred third where things
only seem black or white.

August 6

Today I choose to rest.

August 7

Today I choose joy in every moment.

August 8

Today I choose to expect miracles.

August 9

Today I choose to look for opportunities to connect to people.

August 10

Today I choose to lean into synchronicity.

August 11

Today I choose to look at all of the places
in myself that I feel unrest and drop peace
into those spots and let it ripple
throughout my being.

August 12

Today I choose to expect
good things to happen.

August 13

Today I choose to be at peace.

August 14

Today I choose to lean into kindness and compassion, especially when it feels hard to do.

August 15

Today I choose patience and understanding.

August 16

Today I choose gratitude for all of the amazing modes of transportation that easily and effortlessly take us to visit friends and family and return us safely back home.

August 17

Today I choose to be gentle with my ego as it's really wanting to be heard. I listen to what my ego is really trying to tell me and allow my heart to guide it.

August 18

Today I choose love again and again and
again - Only LOVE!

August 19

Today I choose to have faith and trust that
everything is unfolding in the
Divine perfect plan.

August 20

Today I choose to let others take
responsibility for their actions
and not bail them out.

August 21

Today I choose to use this new moon and solar eclipse energy to release some limiting beliefs that no longer serve me.

August 22

Today I choose to embrace new
beginnings with joy, simplicity and light.

August 23

Today I choose simplicity.

August 24

Today I choose to be gentle with my body
and listen to what it needs.

August 25

Today I choose to take things slowly.

August 26

Today I choose to look for inspiration in unexpected places.

August 27

Today I choose to create a little magic.

August 28

Today I choose to stay centered in my
heart no matter what is going on
outside of me.

August 29

Today I choose to keep leaning into LOVE. I choose to surrender fear and let LOVE alchemize into peace.

August 30

Today I choose to rise to the occasion.

August 31

Today I choose to celebrate the amazing beings in my life.

September 1

Today I choose to recognize the Divine
perfection in everyone I meet.

September 2

Today I choose to lean into Love.

September 3

Today I choose to trust that I know exactly
what to do in any given moment.

September 4

Today I choose to feel the fear
and do it anyway.

September 5

Today I choose to be of service.

September 6

Today I choose to bring Grace
to every challenge I face.

September 7

Today I choose to stay calm and prayerful
for family and friends.

September 8

Today I choose to radiate Love and Peace
from the center of my being blanketing
Mother Earth with Love and Peace.

September 9

Today I choose to radiate peace,
love, and compassion.

September 10

Today I choose to hold fast to prayer and peace.

September 11

Today I choose to have faith and trust that all is well. I continue to lean into Spirit when fear and concern creep in. I center myself in the know that Spirit is always for me.

September 12

Today I choose to be
grounded and peaceful.

September 13

Today I choose to ask, "What is mine to do
today?" and listen for the answer
before I move into action.

September 14

Today I choose to be deliberate
with my every word and action.

September 15

Today I choose simplicity.

September 16

Today I choose to be in the moment.

September 17

Today I choose to enjoy every minute.

September 18

Today I choose to be patient with myself.

September 19

Today I choose to be slow and deliberate.

September 20

Today I choose gratitude for all the miracles and blessings in my life.

September 21

Today I choose to go with the flow.

September 22

Today I choose to pause at this turn of the wheel, reflect on what I'm harvesting and feel into what is wanting to emerge in this new season.

September 23

Today I choose to know that I am
operating in timelessness.

September 24

Today I choose to embrace the fullness of the day.

September 25

Today I choose to have faith in the goodness and kindness of people.

September 26

Today I choose to handle everything with a Light touch.

September 27

Today I choose to honor the beauty and abundance all around me.

September 28

Today I choose to be willing and available
to receive the abundance that is
flowing my way.

September 29

Today I choose to be very clear
with my boundaries.

September 30

Today I choose to trust the Universe...
even when I can't see exactly
where it's guiding me.

October 1

Today I choose to remember
I always have a choice.

October 2

Today I choose to be vigilant in my prayers for peace in myself and peace in our world.

October 3

Today I choose to take one step
toward my dreams.

October 4

Today I choose to listen.

October 5

Today I choose to allow the light
to illuminate the shadows of my soul.

October 6

Today I choose to allow Grace
to guide my day.

October 7

Today I choose joy in all I do.

October 8

Today I choose to look for messages
in the beauty of nature.

October 9

Today I choose to know that
we are Divinely protected.

October 10

Today I choose to have faith and listen for what is mine to do to help friends in need.

October 11

Today I choose to keep leaning into Love and away from fear. I choose to stay in my body, to be calm, to be centered and grounded. I choose to act and speak from that place despite the fear and chaos appearing before me. I choose Love again and again and again.

October 12

Today I choose to make the most of a bad
situation by doing some fun
things with friends.

October 13

Today I choose to keep myself grounded,
to stay present to this now moment and
radiate Love in the face
of fear and uncertainty.

October 14

Today I choose to stay centered in Love
and honor all of the emotions that are
occurring within me and
everyone around me.

October 15

Today I choose gratitude for Life.

October 16

Today I choose to snuggle up
with the people I love.

October 17

Today I choose to keep myself centered in
Love.... again and again and again.

October 18

Today I choose to ride the waves of emotion flowing through me, allowing each feeling to inform me without judgement of what I need in the moment.

October 19

Today I choose to find the order
to what seems to be chaos.

October 20

Today I choose to move at a pace
that soothes my soul.

October 21

Today I choose to allow peace and
stillness to guide my day.

October 22

Today I choose to be patient.

October 23

Today I choose to simply show up.

October 24

Today I choose to do the best I can
and know that it's enough.

October 25

Today I choose to do one thing at a time.

October 26

Today I choose to create.

October 27

Today I choose compassion.

October 28

Today I choose to speak my truth.

October 29

Today I choose to laugh at myself.

October 30

Today I choose gratitude for
every breath I take.

October 31

Today I choose to dance
between the worlds.

November 1

Today I choose to anchor myself
in peace and Love.

November 2

Today I choose to speak to myself with only words of loving kindness.

November 3

Today I choose to hold those I love a little closer to my heart.

November 4

Today I choose gratitude for the beauty all around me.

November 5

Today I choose to be ok with my mind
questioning everything AND
I choose to be still so I can hear my heart's
wisdom and truth.

November 6

Today I choose to focus and listen.

November 7

Today I choose to listen to the
whispers of my soul.

November 8

Today I choose to allow Spirit to
guide me with ease and joy.

November 9

Today I choose to create something new.

November 10

Today I choose to question my motives for
doing things to ensure I'm aligned with
my heart's desires and my soul's purpose.

November 11

Today I choose peace.

November 12

Today I choose to radiate compassion and
honor each beings' path.

November 13

Today I choose to know that there is more than enough... more than enough money, more than enough time, more than enough support, more than enough knowledge, more than enough connection to Spirit... my presence is enough.

November 14

Today I choose to embrace my passions regardless of what anyone else thinks.

November 15

Today I choose to embrace my inner jester.

November 16

Today I choose to simplify.

November 17

Today I choose to take deep breaths and allow my breath to move my emotions.

November 18

Today I choose to embrace life.

November 19

Today I choose LOVE.

November 20

Today I choose to celebrate the
beauty all around me.

November 21

Today I choose to make a difference.

November 22

Today I choose to embrace what ever
Mother Nature has in store.

November 23

Today I choose to be calm.

November 24

Today I choose to speak
with loving kindness.

November 25

Today I choose to let stress go
and embrace my breath.

November 26

Today I choose to forgive.

November 27

Today I choose to make peace
with my past.

November 28

Today I choose to give thanks for Life.

November 29

Today I choose to turn the page
and write a new story.

November 30

Today I choose to walk consciously
through my day.

December 1

Today I choose to look at everything
with the eyes of a child.

December 2

Today I choose to have fun.

December 3

Today I choose to feel like a Star.

December 4

Today I choose to walk in nature.

December 5

Today I choose to be
fiercely compassionate.

December 6

Today I choose self care.

December 7

Today I choose to use my sacred, "No!"

December 8

Today I choose to remember the answers
are within me.

December 9

Today I choose to love my perceived
"imperfections."

December 10

Today I choose to see, feel and be the harmony in my life.

December 11

Today I choose to radiate compassion
and honor each beings' path.

December 12

Today I choose rest.

December 13

Today I choose to do random
acts of kindness.

December 14

Today I chose to be open to new
opportunities.

December 15

Today I choose to feel the oneness
with everyone I meet.

December 16

Today I choose stillness despite the
swirl around me.

December 17

Today I choose to ask,
"What's mine to do?"

December 18

Today I choose to surrender and
allow Grace to do the heavy lifting.

December 19

Today I choose to know that I CAN!

December 20

Today I choose to be conscious of the words I speak after "I am…"

December 21

Today I choose to honor sacred, ancient traditions. Happy Solstice!

December 22

Today I choose to be mindful of my energy levels and rest when needed.

December 23

Today I choose to trust in the
perfection of the day.

December 24

Today I choose to celebrate
Infinite Possibility.

December 25

Today I choose to be present.

December 26

Today I choose to remember I am
made of stardust.

December 27

Today I choose to allow.

December 28

Today I choose to be still so that I can
hear my Spirit's whispers.

December 29

Today I choose to know that
I am enough just as I am.

December 30

Today I choose to appreciate
the small wonders.

December 31

Today I choose to sit on the cusp of wonderful new possibilities and open my heart and mind to what's possible for the new year.

ABOUT MELISSA BINGHAM

Melissa Bingham is a spiritual mentor, intuitive guide and author who helps spiritual seekers unlock the magic of intentional living.

You can learn more about Melissa at her website:

http://todayichoose.me

CONNECT

PODCAST
Coming in early 2021, the *Today I Choose* podcast features interview with inspiring, intentional people, mediations and Melissa's teachings. Find *Today I Choose* on your favorite podcast platform.

JOIN THE COMMUNITY
Visit our website **www.todayichoose.me** to sign up to receive emails about our weekly live meditations, class and more.

FACEBOOK:
Join other intention setters in our Facebook group *Everyday Living with Intention*.